Destination Detectives

Brazil

North
America

Europe

Asia

BRAZIL

Africa

South
America

Australasia

Ali Brownlie Bojang

Raintree

www.raintreepublishers.co.uk
Visit our website to find out more information about **Raintree** books.

To order:
☎ Phone 44 (0) 1865 888112
🗎 Send a fax to 44 (0) 1865 314091
💻 Visit the Raintree Bookshop at **www.raintreepublishers.co.uk** to browse our catalogue and order online.

Produced for Raintree by
White-Thomson Publishing Ltd,
Bridgewater Business Centre,
210 High Street, Lewes, BN7 2NH

First published in Great Britain by Raintree,
Halley Court, Jordan Hill, Oxford OX2 8EJ,
Part of Harcourt Education.
Raintree is a registered trademark of
Harcourt Education Ltd.

Editorial: Sonya Newland, Melanie Waldron,
and Lucy Beevor
Design: Clare Nicholas
Picture Research: Amy Sparks
Production: Chloe Bloom

Originated by Modern Age
Printed and bound in China
By South China Printing Company

10 digit ISBN 1406203084
13 digit ISBN 9781406203080
10 9 8 7 6 5 4 3 2 1
11 10 09 08 07 06

British Library Cataloguing in Publication Data
Brownlie Bojang, Ali, 1949-
    Brazil. - (Destination Detectives)
    1. Brazil. - Geography - Juvenile literature 2. Brazil -
    Social life and customs - 21st century - Juvenile literature
    3. Brazil - Civilisation - Juvenlie literature
    I. Title
    981'.065

Acknowledgements
Corbis pp. 6b (Sergio Pitamitz), 9 (Paulo Fridman), 10–11
(Pierre Merimee), 18 (Archivo Iconografico, S.A.), 20–21
(Jeremy Horner), 21 (Jamil Bittar/Reuters), 22 (Reuters),
25b (Stephanie Maze), 26 (Silvio Avila/Reuters), 33 (Fabio
Polenghi), 36 (Ricardo Azoury); Corbis Sygma pp. 8 (Collart
Herve), 12 (Collart Herve), 14; Photolibrary pp. 4–5 (Jon
Arnold Images), 5t (Index Stock Imagery), 5m (Berndt
Fischer), 5b (Workbook, Inc.), 6t (Berndt Fischer), 11
(Olivier Grunewald), 13 (Digital Vision), 15 (Jon Arnold
Images), 16 (Olivier Grunewald), 17 (Jon Arnold Images),
23 (Workbook, Inc.), 24 (Jon Arnold Images), 25t (Index
Stock Imagery), 28, 38 (Edward Parker), 40 (Berndt
Fischer), 41t (Olivier Grunewald), 41b (Olivier Grunewald);
South American Pictures pp. 19 (Tony Morrison), 27 (Jason
P. Howe), 29 (Tony Morrison), 30 (Tony Morrison), 31
(Tony Morrison), 32 (Tony Morrison), 34 (Tony Morrison),
37 (Tony Morrison), 39 (Tony Morrison), 42 (Tony
Morrison); TopFoto pp. 35, 43.

Cover photograph of Rio Carnival reproduced
with permission of Photolibrary/Workbook, Inc.

Thanks to Rhian Evans and Simon Scoones

Contents

Any words appearing in the text in bold, **like this**, are explained in the glossary. You can also look out for them in the Word Bank box at the bottom of each page.

Where in the world?

The Sleeping Giant

Some people call Brazil the "Sleeping Giant". It is the fifth-largest country in the world after Russia, Canada, China, and the United States, and it has rich **resources**. One day the Sleeping Giant may wake and play a bigger part on the world stage.

You feel the plane shudder and you open your eyes with a start. You look out of the window and are amazed to see that you are flying alongside green mountains. You glance up and see the **summits** a long way above you! Now the plane is skirting over the ocean and you can see beaches dotted with people, wide palm-tree lined avenues, and luxury mansions.

The brazilwood tree
Brazil got its name from a redwood tree called pau brazil or "brazilwood". The red dye from this tree was used by **Amerindians** to paint their faces. It is the national tree of Brazil.

WORD BANK   **Amerindians** name given to native groups living in South America
resources things a country has that help it to make money

The high-rise buildings of a city centre come into view. How can you possibly land where there are so many buildings? Suddenly the runway rushes up towards you and the plane lands with a gentle bump. You have arrived at Santos Dumont airport, a platform built on reclaimed land jutting out into the sea. This is the second airport for Rio de Janeiro – the most exciting city in Brazil!

Find out later...

Where will you find this giant statue?

Where in Brazil can you see hundreds of rare animals and birds?

Which city hosts the biggest carnival in the world?

Rio de Janeiro has one of the most beautiful natural harbours in the world.

summit highest point of a mountain

Brazil in a nutshell

As you leave the airport you buy a map and a guidebook for a few *real* – the money used in Brazil. You can see straight away that Brazil is the biggest country in South America. You also notice that it lies south of the **Equator**. You begin to make some notes.

Brazil at a glance

SIZE:
8.5 million square kilometres (3.3 million square miles)

CAPITAL:
Brasilia

POPULATION:
186 million

MAIN RELIGION:
Catholic

CURRENCY:
Real, written R$

TYPE OF GOVERNMENT:
Federal republic (see page 7)

The Pantanal is a vast area of wetlands and swamps. It is home to many different **species** of flowers, birds, and animals. These include birds like the hyacinth macaw and the toucan, and the Cayman – a kind of alligator (above).

Giant sand dunes and delicious seafood are key attractions in Natal, in northeastern Brazil.

WORD BANK   Equator imaginary line around the middle of Earth
rainforest warm, wet forest found in a tropical region

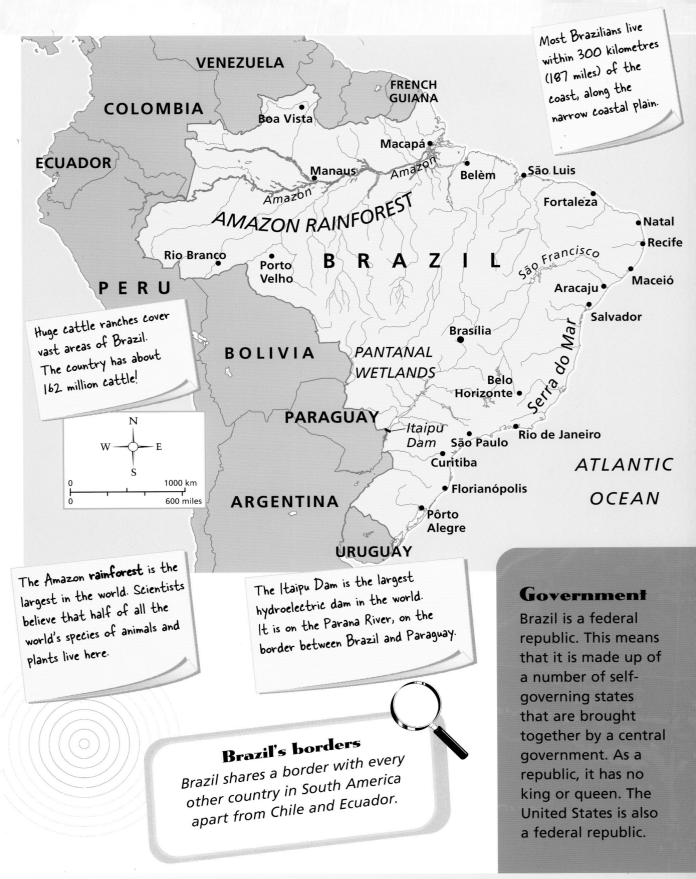

VENEZUELA

COLOMBIA

FRENCH
GUIANA

Boa Vista

ECUADOR

Macapá

Manaus Amazon Belèm São Luis

Amazon

Fortaleza

AMAZON RAINFOREST

Natal

Recife

Rio Branco

B R A Z I L

São Francisco

Maceió

Porto
Velho

Aracaju

P E R U

Salvador

Serra do Mar

Brasília

BOLIVIA

PANTANAL
WETLANDS

Belo
Horizonte

PARAGUAY

Itaipu
Dam

São Paulo

Rio de Janeiro

ATLANTIC

Curitiba

OCEAN

Florianópolis

ARGENTINA

Pôrto
Alegre

URUGUAY

Most Brazilians live within 300 kilometres (187 miles) of the coast, along the narrow coastal plain.

Huge cattle ranches cover vast areas of Brazil. The country has about 162 million cattle!

N
W   E
S

0   1000 km
0   600 miles

The Amazon rainforest is the largest in the world. Scientists believe that half of all the world's species of animals and plants live here.

The Itaipu Dam is the largest hydroelectric dam in the world. It is on the Parana River, on the border between Brazil and Paraguay.

Government
Brazil is a federal republic. This means that it is made up of a number of self-governing states that are brought together by a central government. As a republic, it has no king or queen. The United States is also a federal republic.

Brazil's borders
Brazil shares a border with every other country in South America apart from Chile and Ecuador.

species different types of animals and plants

Getting around

Looking at your map you can see that getting around Brazil is going to be quite a challenge. It is so large that travelling around could take some time. It is not only the vast distances that make travelling difficult, though. In some remote parts of Brazil, there are very few roads, and they can often be in poor condition.

The Trans-Amazonian Highway

The Government has been building new roads to some of the more **remote** areas for over 30 years. It wants to encourage people and new businesses to settle there. The most important of these main roads is the Trans-Amazonian Highway, which provides a route right through the Amazon **rainforest**.

Long-distance travel

Long-distance buses travel to many destinations, and on some of them you can get a sleeper – a seat that stretches out to become a bed. Boat trips are a good way to travel along the Amazon River. On some of these you can even sleep in hammocks on deck!

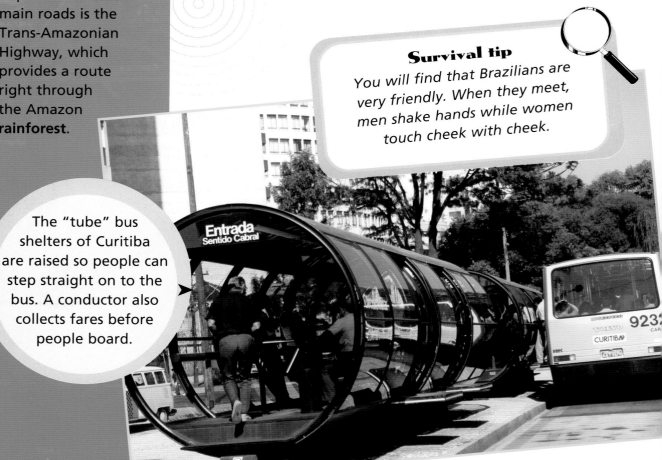

Survival tip

You will find that Brazilians are very friendly. When they meet, men shake hands while women touch cheek with cheek.

The "tube" bus shelters of Curitiba are raised so people can step straight on to the bus. A conductor also collects fares before people board.

Entrada
Sentido Cabral

WORD BANK   remote   far from other places

If you really want to explore the whole of Brazil, though, you will probably have to fly to some places. This is certainly the quickest way of getting from one end of the country to the other – otherwise the journey could take days. Not all Brazilians can afford to fly, however, and most people travel from town to town by bus or car.

Manaus

3,490 km
(2,167 miles)

2,135 km
(1,326 miles)   Recife

Salvador
1,446 km
(898 miles)

N
W   E
S
0   1000 km
0   600 miles

1,015 km
(630 miles)

1,148 km
(713 miles)

São
Paulo

Rio de
Janeiro

The 1,609-kilometre (1,000-mile) long highway linking the Amazon River with southern Brazil.

Brasilia, the capital, is over 1,000 kilometres (600 miles) from any of the other large cities.

Mountain railway

It is possible to take a train to the top of the Corcovado Mountain in Rio de Janeiro. Thousands of people make this trip every year because of the amazing views it offers over the city.

9

Climate & landscape

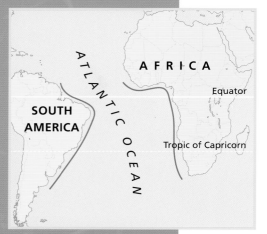

Looking at your map again, you notice how the eastern bulge of Brazil "fits" into the curve of West Africa (see map left). This is not a coincidence. Many millions of years ago, Africa and South America were part of the same **land mass**, but they drifted apart very slowly. Even today, many similar plants and animals are found in these two areas.

The climate

Brazil extends from the **Equator** to the **Tropic of Capricorn**. Its vast size means that the **climate** varies greatly depending on where you are – in the north or south, on the coast, inland, or in the mountains.

El Niño

The dry north-east of Brazil is affected by a **current** in the Pacific Ocean called El Niño. Scientists can tell when the current will affect the weather. When it's an "El Niño year" the farmers know it will rain less so they grow cotton instead of rice.

In the north-east, the landscape is very dry, with only a few shrubs.

▼

Survival tip

Don't forget that Brazil is in the Southern Hemisphere. This means that when it is summer in Europe and the United States, it is winter in Brazil, and vice versa.

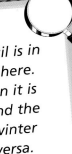

WORD BANK   **drought** period of time without the usual amount of rainfall
humid when there is a lot of water vapour in the air

Tropical **rainforests** cover more than half the country. The climate here hardly changes at all throughout the year. It is always hot, **humid**, and rainy. There is around 2,200 mm (90 inches) of rainfall per year.

In the north-east it can get as hot as 40°C (104°F), but there is little rain, and the area suffers from frequent **droughts**. At these times, the land looks parched and barren.

A light mist rises from the humid rainforest.

Temperature extremes

	Minimum	Maximum
Manaus	18°C (64°F)	36°C (97°F)
Belem	21°C (70°F)	34°C (93°F)
São Paulo	5°C (41°F)	34°C (93°F)
Porto Alegre	−0.2°C (36°F)	37°C (99°F)
Brasilia	7°C (45°F)	32°C (90°F)

land mass large, unbroken area of land
Tropic of Capricorn imaginary line that marks 23° south of the Equator

Manaus

You are here!

N W E S

0 — 1000 km
0 — 600 miles

The Amazon rainforest

You pack a few clothes and catch a flight to Manaus, a city in the heart of Amazonia. From here you take a boat and begin your journey along the magnificent Amazon River!

The Amazon is the second-longest river in the world, after the Nile. It flows for over 6,275 kilometres (3,890 miles) from its source in the Andes Mountains in Peru, through the vast **rainforest**, to the Atlantic Ocean.

Healing plants

Many of the 55,000 plant **species** found in the Brazilian rainforest are used in Western medicines. For example, quinine is used to treat **malaria**, and other plants are used to treat Parkinson's disease and eye diseases.

Fast fact
The mouth of the Amazon is over 320 kilometres (200 miles) wide.

The Mucajai River, carrying lots of **silt**, winds its way through the Amazon rainforest.

WORD BANK canopy covering provided by the tops of trees in forests
dengue fever disease spread by Aedes mosquitoes

Your boat moors at a small jetty and your guide takes you for a walk through the forest. The light is dim under the dense **canopy**. There are many insects in the dark undergrowth, including mosquitoes and ants. Leafcutter ants chew leaves and mix them with their own saliva. Fungus then grows on the chewed leaves, providing food for the ants and their young.

The hot, **humid** conditions make the rainforest the perfect home for thousands of **species** of plants and animals. Some are very rare and can only be found in the rainforest.

Over the last 40 years, the rainforest has been badly damaged by people cutting down and burning the trees to make room for roads and farming.

Millions of trees in the rainforest have been cut down to make way for mining and quarrying.

malaria disease spread by infected Anopheles mosquitoes
silt soil, mud, or clay that builds up in a river

The Yanomami

The Yanomami people are one of the tribes that live in the Amazon rainforest. They believe that river and forest spirits guide their lives and that it is important to live in harmony with the forest. However, they are under constant threat as they lose their traditional lands to farming or mining.

Life in the rainforest

You walk on through the **rainforest** and come across a small settlement of **Amerindians**. The women are weaving baskets while the men are huddled round a radio. Your guide introduces you to a young woman.

She tells you that just twenty years ago all her family lived in small settlements like this one, moving around from year to year to grow their crops of bananas, **manioc**, and maize on new land. There were no shops, no schools, and no houses. Her family survived by farming, hunting, and fishing for what they needed. In the 1970s, the Government encouraged newcomers to settle here by building new roads and by setting up new villages and towns. Since then, large areas have been cleared and much of the rainforest has been destroyed. Life has been difficult for her family.

The Yanomami people like to paint their faces and bodies with lines, dots, and circles. ➤

WORD BANK manioc type of root vegetable
export selling goods to other countries

Mining

The Greater Carajas mine in the Amazon rainforest is one of the largest **open-cast mines** in the world. It produces iron ore, manganese, copper, tin, and even gold. Some local Amerindian people feel their land is being taken away from them. Small farmers, large ranches producing cattle for beef, and big farms producing soy are taking over large areas of land.

Manaus is the starting point for many tourist boat trips along the Amazon River. People sleep in hammocks on deck or in cabins.

Manaus

Manaus is one of the world's largest river ports. Farming products and thousands of tons of electronics and other products made in Manaus are **exported** every day. Manaus holds 50 percent of Amazonia's three million inhabitants, the rest of the population lives in very small Amerindian villages throughout the forest.

open-cast mining where a large hole is dug rather than tunnelling underground to find minerals

The Planalto Brasileiro

The rest of Brazil's landscape is very varied, and much of the scenery is stunning.

Most of Brazil south of the Amazon Basin is a vast **plateau**, known as the Planalto Brasileiro. This includes open plains and cattle ranches. Brazil produces more beef than any other country. This area is bordered to the east by the Serra do Mar mountain range, which falls into the narrow coastal belt, where cities like Rio de Janeiro and Vitória are located. To the south-west of the plateau is an area of waterfalls, deep canyons, and high rolling grasslands.

Turtles on the coast

Brazil has nearly 7,500 kilometres (4,660 miles) of coastline. Five **species** of turtle can be found here, including the green, loggerhead, hawksbill, olive ridley, and giant turtles. These are all protected by law. Illegal fishing with nets along the coast and industrial fishing have placed the turtles at risk.

Turtles head back towards the sea on one of Brazil's beaches.

WORD BANK   fertile   land that is good for growing crops

Wetlands

In the far west, the Pantanal is a massive area of wetlands on the border with Bolivia and Paraguay. It is almost ten times the size of the Everglades in Florida, United States. Like the Amazon, it has a rich amount of birds, animals, and plants. Here you can find the beautiful hyacinth macaw – the world's largest parrot – as well as giant river otters and jaguars.

The Caatinga

The least **fertile** area in Brazil is the Caatinga – an area of dry, stony, barren scrubland in the north-east of the country. Farmers have to work hard here to make a living. In the far south, pine forests and grasslands complete the picture of Brazil's varied landscapes.

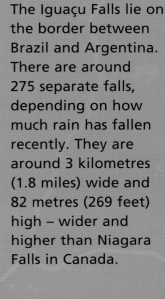

Iguaçu Falls

The Iguaçu Falls lie on the border between Brazil and Argentina. There are around 275 separate falls, depending on how much rain has fallen recently. They are around 3 kilometres (1.8 miles) wide and 82 metres (269 feet) high – wider and higher than Niagara Falls in Canada.

Fast fact
The highest point in Brazil is Pico da Neblina, at 3,014 metres (9,889 feet).

The different waterfalls that make up the Iguaçu Falls are separated by rocky islands.

plateau   fairly high, flat area of land

History & culture

Amerindians of the rainforest

There are around 330,000 **Amerindians** spread between more than 200 different groups living in the **rainforest**. They speak 180 languages or dialects, and have their own religions and customs. Today, they make up less than 1 percent of Brazil's total population.

Back in Manaus you notice what a mix of people there is. The **Amerindians** you met in the **rainforest** are descended from Brazil's first people. The earliest settlers in Brazil probably came from Asia many thousands of years ago. They were here when the Portuguese arrived in 1500.

Portuguese influence

The Portuguese made Brazil a **colony**. They began cultivating the land and found they needed people to help them, especially on the large sugar plantations they set up. Between the mid-16th and 17th centuries they brought millions of slaves over the Atlantic Ocean from West Africa. These slaves brought with them their own types of food, music, and religion. These have all shaped the culture of much of Brazil today.

An 18th-century painting showing slaves mining diamonds, watched over by their European masters.

WORD BANK   colony country taken over by another country as part of an empire

Multicultural Brazil

In the 19th century, the rulers of Brazil encouraged people from Europe to move to their country by offering them small plots of land. Many newcomers worked in the coffee industry and in gold mining in Brazil. Between 1909 and 1972, many Asians, particularly Japanese people, came to Brazil to work on small farms around São Paulo.

Today, Brazil's population is a rich mix of people from all over the world – Amerindians, Africans, Europeans, and Asians.

Ethnic divisions

Caucasian (mainly European): 54 percent

Mixed race: 39 percent

African: 6 percent

Other (Japanese, Arab, Amerindian): 1 percent

Survival tip

Today nearly everyone in Brazil speaks Portuguese as their main language. It is the language used in schools, newspapers, radio, and television. Brazilians love it if you try to speak a few words in Portuguese.

São Paulo has the largest population of Japanese people outside Japan.

Amerindian music

The music of the Amerindians is less well known than Brazilian dance music. The Amerindians take the sounds that they hear in the **rainforest** and imitate them in their music. For musical instruments they use rattles, drums, whistles, reed flutes, and horns.

Music and dance

Nearly all aspects of Brazilian culture have been shaped by this wonderful mix of European, African, **Amerindian**, and Asian traditions. This is especially so for music and dance, and in Brazil you cannot separate the two. Over 500 years, the mix of European and African musical styles has created a type of music that is purely Brazilian.

The Europeans contributed instruments such as the guitar and songs like ballads; Africans the drums and percussion instruments, and the heavy, complicated rhythms known as poly rhythms. Sometimes the music is cool and laid-back, like the gentle dance rhythms of the bosso nova and samba. At other times it is loud and raucous, and makes you feel good to be alive!

A band of drummers in Bahia is known as a *bateria*.

martial art   form of self-defence, often practised as a sport or an art

You hear music everywhere you go in Brazil, from street corners to cafés. People are always dancing – young and old, black and white, rich and poor. It might be a child dancing in the street as music blares out from someone's radio, or an old man sitting tapping his feet in time to the beat as he sips his strong Brazilian coffee.

You hear that there is a great exhibition of music and dance in Rio de Janeiro – the famous Carnival – so that's where you decide to head next.

Students demonstrate capoeira in front of the Brazilian National Congress building in Brasilia.

Capoeira

Capoeira is a mix of **martial arts** and dancing with music and song. It started in the African country of Angola. The contestants move in a series of cartwheels and handstands, trying to deliver blows to each other using only their legs, feet, heels, and heads. This is all done in time to music.

The day of the Carnival

In Rio de Janeiro, you make your way to the Sambodromo. This is a massive stadium, 700 metres (half a mile) long, built on either side of a wide avenue, down which the carnival procession passes. Your seat is way up high, and you have a bird's-eye view.

The Carnival begins at dusk. Samba schools compete with each other, and only the best from the previous year get to join the main procession. They spend months building their parade floats, practising their dancing, and making wonderfully elaborate costumes. Everyone gets very excited.

A spectacular samba school float in the Sambodromo carnival stadium.

▼

fasting   going without food for a period of time

Each school is led out by the leader, blowing a wooden whistle called an *apitos*. The bands play and the drums pound – the noise is deafening and there's no way you can have a conversation. You cheer and laugh until your face and sides ache. Nearly all cities in Brazil have their own parade, but everyone agrees that Rio de Janeiro's is the best.

In the evening, you wander through the city, where smaller street parades are taking place. Before you know what has happened, you have joined in with the biggest party in the world.

An old festival
The first records of a carnival in Rio de Janeiro date back to 1723. In those early days, people went out into the streets and poured buckets of water and threw limes at each other. People marched through the streets banging drums and tambourines, and blowing whistles.

Survival tip
You are allowed to throw tomatoes during the Carnival – but they must already be squashed so that they don't harm anyone!

Carnival participants wear fabulous costumes.

Religion

Tucked in-between office blocks in the city centre, you have noticed many old churches, some dating back to the 16th century. Many were built by Christian Portuguese **immigrants**, who brought Catholicism to Brazil. Today, over 70 percent of the population is Catholic. Many people mix beliefs from different religions in with Catholicism.

Candomblé

Candomblé combines the rituals of a religion brought by Yoruba slaves from Nigeria, West Africa, with Catholicism and **Amerindian** customs. Followers of this religion believe that everyone has one or two spirits called orixás that are responsible for the kind of person they are.

The modern architecture of the Metropolitan Cathedral in Brasilia.

Religion in Brazil

Catholic: 70 percent
Protestant: 15 percent
Other (African religions, Jews, Muslims, Buddhists): 2 percent
No religion: 13 percent

They also believe in Jesus, and make offerings to the spirits and Jesus at the same time. Services include a lot of drumming and dancing. Candomblé is followed mostly by Afro-Brazilians in Bahia state.

Some African beliefs involve leaving offerings of chicken, flowers, and candles at crossroads, on beaches, and other public places. Customs like this are followed on festivals like Iemanjá, on New Year's Eve.

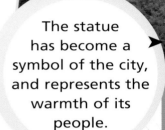

The statue has become a symbol of the city, and represents the warmth of its people.

Christ the Redeemer

Rio de Janeiro is overlooked by a giant statue of Jesus, called Christ the Redeemer. It stands on Corcovado Mountain. Built in 1931, the statue is 30 metres (98 feet) high – just a little bit shorter than the Statue of Liberty in New York.

Girls celebrating the festival of Iemanjá on New Year's Eve. Iemanjá is a mother goddess. Flowers and perfume are brought to the beach and thrown into the sea.

25

Everyday life

Pelé – the Black Pearl

Pelé was one of the best-known soccer players in the world. He was also known as the "Black Pearl", but his real name is Edson Arantes do Nascimento. He scored more than 1,200 goals during his career. Brazilian footballers are often just known by one name, like Pelé and Ronaldo.

You decide to spend a day on one of Rio de Janeiro's amazing beaches with your friends. This is clearly the place to be – it seems like everyone is here! You hire a parasol to shade you from the hot sun, and buy some drinks from a vendor on the beach. You can buy anything here – from swimwear and sunglasses to Brazilian flags and pots.

A group of young people are playing volleyball and others are surfing in the waves. Outdoor sports are very popular with Brazilians. Brazil's men's team won the gold medals for indoor and beach volleyball in the 2004 Athens Olympics. The women's team won silver for beach volleyball. Basketball, tennis, and canoeing are also popular sports.

The volleyball court on Copacabana Beach.

➤

WORD BANK *surdo* bass drum that marks the beat of samba music

Football mad

In the evening you go to a football match in the massive Maracana stadium in Rio de Janeiro – the biggest football stadium in the world. This is where you can really see how passionate Brazilians are about football – or *futebol* as they call it in Portuguese. The crowd is awash with yellow shirts, and throughout the match there is the booming of a big *surdo* drum. People wave their flags and cheer. Every time Brazil scores, the band plays and firecrackers go off!

Motor racing

Motor racing is another popular sport in Brazil. Many Formula One racing drivers are Brazilian, including Rubens Barrichello and world champions Nelson Piquet, Ayrton Senna, and Emerson Fittipaldi.

Brazilian football fans cheer on their team in the Maracana stadium.

Fast fact
The Brazilian football team has won the World Cup for soccer an amazing five times – in 1958, 1962, 1970, 1994, and 2002.

Food

Feijoada is Brazil's national dish. It is made from pork with black beans, cooked in a big pot and served with rice and cabbage. The African slaves were the first people to make this dish. They took the leftovers from their owners' meals and created a new dish.

Food from Bahia state has been strongly influenced by African cooking, and is quite spicy. Dishes include *vatapa* (shrimps cooked in coconut milk), *sarapatel* (liver with tomatoes, peppers, and onions), and *caruru* (shrimps with okra, onions, and peppers). *Moqueca* is a seafood stew, flavoured with palm oil and coconut milk.

Bob's restaurant

Although Brazil has many American-owned fast-food restaurants, a local chain called Bob's is a favourite. This hot-dog and hamburger restaurant started in the early 1950s. It has 388 outlets, and is the second-largest food chain in Brazil, after McDonalds.

Eating habits

Brazilians usually have their main meal in the middle of the day, around 1 p.m., and eat again late in the evening, around 9 p.m.

Feijoada – Brazil's national dish. A traditional *feijoada* is made with every part of the pig!

WORD BANK   marinated soaked in spices and flavourings before cooking

Barbequed meat is also a favourite in Brazil, where it is known as *churrasco*. The meat, which can be chicken, pork, or beef, is usually **marinated** in oil and garlic for a few hours before being grilled. It is served with rice and *farofa* – seasoned **manioc** flour.

Survival tip

It is very rude in Brazil to eat food when walking down the street – even take-away food. It should be eaten where you bought it, or taken home.

Daily doughnuts

Bolinho de chuva are traditional doughnuts found all over Brazil. They are served at breakfast or tea time. You can have them salty with green onions, or sweet. They are best eaten when they are very fresh.

A woman selling traditional snacks on the street-side.

Going to school

You get up very early the next morning. Your friends have to be at school by 7 a.m.! You have breakfast of bread rolls with butter, jam, and white cheese, followed by some papaya. They leave promptly at 6.45 a.m. in their smart school uniforms for the short walk to their schools.

Primary-school children often attend either in the morning or the afternoon, rather than both. Children start school when they are seven years old and learn maths, geography, and history – much the same as schools in the United Kingdom and Australia. All children are taught in Portuguese.

Children leaving a secondary school in the city of Cuiabá, in western Brazil.

English is taught at secondary schools and pupils also learn about computers. An average school has about 1,000 pupils. They have to work hard to pass exams at the end of the year. If they don't, they have to do the year all over again.

Amerindian schooling

Amerindians have their own education system, where children, mainly boys, learn their traditions from the elders.

State and private schools

State schools in Brazil do not receive a great deal of money, and teachers are not well paid. There might be 40 pupils in a class. Schools in the country are even poorer than those in the cities. Many parents now try to send their children to private schools, but this is expensive.

A primary school in the poor suburb of Juazeiro do Norte.

Cities of Brazil

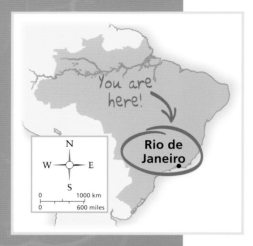

You are here!

Rio de Janeiro

N W E S

0 — 1000 km
0 — 600 miles

Many people have told you that Rio de Janeiro is one of the most beautiful cities in the world. It is a wonderful clear day, so you take the opportunity to go to the top of Corcovado Mountain.

The view is breathtaking. Lying below you is a city of over 11 million people. The city is wedged between the bay, the ocean, and the mountains – with long thin strips reaching out along the narrow coastal plain. Space is very limited, so most of the buildings are tall and crammed together.

Growing cities

Nearly 80 percent of Brazilians live in cities (in 1950 it was 36 percent). Cities have grown rapidly over the last 30 years, as people have come from other countries or moved in from the countryside. Brazil has some of the largest cities in the world.

Favelas

You notice the favelas, or slums, creeping up the hillsides behind the city. These are settlements of **makeshift** houses where the poor live. These are usually people who have come to Rio de Janeiro from the countryside, looking for work.

A typical Brazilian favela.

WORD BANK makeshift something that has been put together quickly

Most cities in Brazil have favelas, and the Government is now trying to improve them. They ask the people who live in the favelas how they want their communities to develop. The Government has also installed street lighting, sewage systems, and waste-disposal systems. Community centres have also been built in many areas.

City locations

Most of Brazil's towns and cities are located in the south-east and the south. People have been moving here from areas in the north-east. Nevertheless, there are some large cities in the north-east, including Salvador and Recife.

Soccer is a national passion, and children of all ages play it, in the streets and the favelas.

Fast fact

Twelve cities in Brazil have populations of over one million.

Curitiba

The southern city of Curitiba has one of the most efficient bus systems in the world. Express buses rush **commuters** in and out of the city centre. Bus stops are specially designed so that people can get on and off buses quickly, and are easy for disabled people to use (see page 8).

Street children

One of the first things you notice in Brazilian cities are the street children. There is no **welfare system**, so poor families often have to send their children out to beg. Sometimes they earn money by washing car windscreens at traffic lights or cleaning shoes while you wait.

The other thing you notice about the cities is how busy and noisy they are. Cars are bumper to bumper and pump out exhaust fumes that pollute the air. Drivers often pass the time listening to music on their radios.

These street children make money by polishing people's shoes.

commuter person who travels to and from work
futuristic very modern – as it might be in the future

Other cities

Brasilia was designed in the shape of an aeroplane, with north and south wings, and was built in the 1950s. It was an attempt to open up the centre of the country. It has **futuristic** buildings and wide roads. It took over as the capital from Rio de Janeiro in 1960.

São Paulo

São Paulo is an enormous, sprawling city of about 20 million people. It is the largest city in Brazil, and one of the largest in the world. It is a major business and industrial centre.

Salvador

Salvador, in the north-east, has the largest concentration of people of African descent. It was the centre of the slave trade and the sugar-cane industry. It is a large, modern city, but you can still see the evidence of its past.

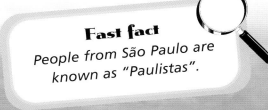

The skyscrapers of São Paulo stretch out to the horizon.

welfare system   scheme to help people with no money

Living in the countryside

Brazil has big, busy cities, as you have discovered. However, there are also large areas of the country where very few people live. What is life like in these **rural** areas? Farming is the main source of income for the people who live in the countryside.

An awful lot of coffee...

Many crops are grown in Brazil to sell to other countries. These are known as cash crops. Sugar was one of the earliest of this type of crop. Then coffee became very profitable and some people grew very rich as a result. "They grow an awful lot of coffee in Brazil" is a line from an old song – and it's true. Brazil still produces more coffee beans than any other country, and provides 40 percent of the world's coffee. It grows mainly in the areas around São Paulo and Rio de Janeiro.

Agriculture in São Paulo

The state of São Paulo has a successful farming industry. It produces most of Brazil's oranges – and Brazil produces more than any other country. It also produces half of its sugar, 40 percent of its chickens and eggs, and 20 percent of its coffee.

Fast fact
Seventy-five percent of the oranges produced in Brazil are turned into orange juice.

A man picking coffee beans. In the 19th century, coffee took the place of sugar as Brazil's most important crop.

WORD BANK poncho square or oblong piece of material with an opening for the head

Over the past few years, soybeans have become Brazil's most important crop for **export**. However, crops like coffee and soybeans are not the only things that Brazilian land is good for. In the south and central areas of Brazil are huge open grasslands – known as pampa. These parts are ideal for cattle rearing and there are many large ranches here. Beef has become one of Brazil's most important exports.

In total, twenty percent of the people of Brazil work in these different types of farming.

Gauchos are Brazil's equivalent to American cowboys. Brazil exports 550,000 tons of beef a year – most of it to Europe.

Gauchos

In Brazil, the name for a cowboy who rounds up the cattle on horseback is a gaucho. They traditionally wore a wide hat, a **poncho**, and knee-high leather boots. They travelled from ranch to ranch, wherever there was work. Gauchos still play an important role on Brazil's ranches.

rural relating to the countryside

In the poor north-east, new projects are helping people to help themselves by developing simple, cheap ways of saving water. Farmers dig small dams to capture precious rainwater to **irrigate** their fields. These schemes are helping farmers provide food for themselves and their families.

The poorest parts of Brazil are found in the north-east. Small villages are inhabited by farmers and their families, who have to make a living out of the parched, dry land. They mainly farm vegetables and fruit for themselves, or grow cotton to sell. In **drought** years it is difficult to grow anything apart from cacti! Many people leave the countryside to look for work in the cities.

Minerals

Many minerals are mined in the countryside. Iron ore, bauxite – which is used to make aluminium, which in turn is used to make cans – and manganese, are all important minerals.

As Brazil grows, it needs more energy, particularly oil to fuel cars and machinery. Oil has been pumped from deepwater fields off the coast since the 1970s. This has produced half its energy needs. However, Brazil cannot provide all the energy it needs, and has to **import** the rest from other countries.

A farmer harvests sugar cane in the poor north-eastern region of Brazil.

WORD BANK   import buy in goods from other countries

Fishing

Fish is a popular food in Brazil. Most of it is fished by small independent fisher folk. There are a few fishing businesses that use modern equipment. Fishing is also a popular tourist activity.

Fishermen bring their catch of shrimps ashore at Peba, a small town by the Atlantic Ocean.

US immigrants

In the last few years, more than 200 US farmers, mainly from the Midwest, have moved to Brazil. They have sold their US farms and joined with others to buy farms in Brazil. Land is much cheaper there than it is in the United States.

irrigate artificially supply water for farming

Environment & wildlife

The tamarin

The golden-headed lion tamarin is a small monkey. It is so-called because its fur looks like a lion's mane. Its natural **habitat** is the Atlantic forest of north-east Brazil, but less than one-tenth of the original forest remains, and the tamarin is close to **extinction**. There may be only around 200 left.

You're coming near to the end of your stay in Brazil. You go to a café with your Brazilian friends and they tell you how they feel about their country.

They believe they live in one of the most beautiful countries in the world, but they have some concerns for the future of its land and its animals. They think more needs to be done to protect them.

Protecting the rainforest

The **rainforest** is one of the most threatened areas of Brazil. Trees have been cut down to make way for ranches, for mines, and dams. Cattle ranching is the leading cause of **deforestation**. The number of cattle in the Amazon doubled during the 1990s, but when ranches replace the forest, the soil quickly dries up. Some say that the land becomes more like a desert after just ten years.

Amazon animals
The Amazon rainforest contains 30 percent of all known plant and animal **species**, including 1,800 species of birds and 250 different mammals.

Tamarin monkeys are very shy. They live high in the tree tops and sleep in holes in the trees.

WORD BANK   **deforestation** when trees are removed from an area
extinction when an animal or a plant no longer exists

The Brazilian Environment Agency, IBAMA, has the job of protecting the rainforest to make sure that people are not damaging it illegally. They have new hi-tech **surveillance** systems to help them – six satellites and eighteen aeroplanes. They have a huge area to watch over.

The tree frog uses its tongue to catch insects. It has suction cups on the bottom of its feet to help it climb trees.

The hyacinth macaw

The hyacinth macaw is the world's largest parrot, and lives in the Pantanal swamps in the west of Brazil. It has bright blue plumage, and some people will pay a lot of money – up to £6,000 – to have one as a pet.

The hyacinth macaw grows to 100 centimetres (40 inches) in length and weighs 1,250 grams (3 pounds).

habitat place where an animal or a plant lives
surveillance keeping something under close observation

Stay or go?

Your stay in Brazil has come to an end. You have seen so much and so many contrasts – between the cities and the countryside, between rich and poor. You have been impressed with the friendliness of the people, and with their love of music and dance and having fun. What would you do if you stayed? There are still so many things to see and do. What's it going to be? Stay or go?

Enjoying nature

There are many natural wonders still to see in Brazil. You could visit the Chapada Diamantina – an area of unusual rock formations, underground rivers, and waterfalls that lies in the north-east of Brazil. Or how about a rock-climbing expedition at Bau Rock in the Mantiqueira Mountains?

Television favourite

One of Brazil's most popular television programmes is called *Malhacao*. This is a soap opera that is especially for young people.

The Opera House in Manaus was built during the rubber boom between 1890 and 1920. The best performers from Europe and North America came to perform here. It has recently been restored.

Another worthwhile day trip is to watch the sun rise over the Pantanal before spending the day bird-watching – a fascinating pastime in Brazil, because there are so many brightly coloured and unusual birds.

Other things to do

- Go to the recently renovated Opera House in Manaus.
- Visit Ouro Preto – the city at the centre of the gold-mining region.
- Take the ferry to the island of Paqueta in Rio de Janeiro bay – a small island with no cars.
- Eat *arroz carreteiro* – "truck driver's rice" – a dish of rice seasoned with dried beef.
- Visit the Museum of Japanese Immigration in São Paulo.

A tourist hotspot

Brazil is a major destination for tourists. Many airlines fly direct to Brazilian cities. Nearly half of all visitors to Brazil pass through Rio de Janeiro.

The city of Recife lies in the north-east of Brazil, on the Atlantic Ocean.

Find out more

Destination Detectives can find out more about Brazil by using the books and websites listed below.

World Wide Web

If you want to find out more about Brazil you can search the Internet using keywords such as these:

- Brazil
- Rio de Janeiro
- Brasilia
- Amazon rainforest

You can also find your own keywords by using headings or words from this book. Try using a search directory such as www.google.co.uk.

The Brazilian Embassy

The Brazilian embassy in your own country has lots of information about Brazil. You can find out about the different regions, the best times to visit, special events, and all about Brazilian culture. Embassies in many countries have their own websites. The UK embassy website address is: www.brazil.org.uk.

Further reading

Cassio's Day: From Dawn to Dusk in a Brazilian City by Maria de Fatima Campos (Frances Lincoln, 2001)
Countries of the World: Brazil by Brian Dicks (Evans Brothers, 2002)
Country Files: Brazil by Marion Morrison (Franklin Watts, 2003)
Nations of the World: Brazil by Anita Dalal (Raintree, 2003)
The Changing Face of Brazil by Edward Parker (Hodder Wayland, 2001)
Visit to... Brazil by Peter and Connie Roop (Heinemann, 2003)
World in Focus: Brazil by Simon Scoones (Hodder, 2006)
World Tour: Brazil by Adriana Dominguez (Raintree, 2003)

Timeline

3000 BC
First people arrive, probably from Asia.

1494
Pope Alexander VI gives Brazil to Portugal.

1500
Portuguese arrive and claim the land.

1530
Brazil becomes a Portuguese colony.

1763
Rio de Janeiro becomes the capital of Brazil.

1822
Independence is declared.

1840
Dom Pedro II becomes emperor of Brazil.

1960
The capital city is moved to Brasilia.

1943
Brazil joins the **Allies** against Germany in World War II – the only Latin American country to play an active role in the war.

1890s
A coffee boom brings in a wave of almost one million European immigrants during the 19th century.

1890
Pedro II gives up the throne and Brazil is declared a republic.

1888
Abolition of slavery. Many Europeans start to arrive.

1964–85
Military rule: for 21 years Brazil was ruled by military governments. People were not able to vote and the press was censored.

1977
Brazilian **Amerindians** or native peoples, hold their first national conference.

1992
The United Nations Earth Summit takes place in Rio de Janeiro.

1994
Brazil wins its fourth World Cup in soccer.

2000
Brazil celebrates its 500th anniversary as a country.

2005
President Lula is accused of corruption, reducing his chances of being re-elected in 2006.

2004
Brazil launches its first space rocket.

2003
Lula elected as President of Brazil.

2002
Brazil wins its fifth World Cup in soccer.

45

Brazil – facts & figures

The Brazilian flag shows the night sky in a yellow diamond, sitting on a green background. The green represents all the forests in the country, the yellow diamond represents the minerals that are mined in Brazil. The night sky is that of the Southern Hemisphere. The banner across the circle says in Latin, "Order and Progress".

People and places

- Population: 186 million.
- Life expectancy: men – 68; women – 76.
- Brazil is 4,319 km (2,684 miles) wide at its widest – almost the same distance as it is from north to south – 4,394 kilometres (2,731 miles).
- 20 percent of the world's fresh water is supplied by the Amazon River.

Technology

- It is estimated that in 2005 there were 60 million mobile phones in Brazil.
- There are more mobiles than landlines.
- Internet domain: br.

Money matters

- Chief crops: coffee, sugar cane, soybean, cocoa, beef, wheat, rice, maize.
- Exports: manufactured goods, iron ore, soybeans, footwear, coffee, beef.
- Natural resources: bauxite, gold, iron ore, manganese, nickel.
- Major industries: steel, cars, computers, textiles, shoes, chemicals.
- Brazil is the world's largest exporter of television programmes.

Glossary

Allies the nations that fought against Germany in World War II

Amerindians name given to native groups living in South America

canopy covering provided by the tops of trees in forests

climate general weather conditions in an area

colony country taken over by another country as part of an empire

commuter person who travels to and from work

current steady flow of water

deforestation when trees are removed from an area

dengue fever disease spread by Aedes mosquitoes

drought period of time without the usual amount of rainfall

Equator imaginary line around the middle of Earth

export selling goods to other countries

extinction when an animal or a plant no longer exists

fasting going without food for a period

fertile land that is good for growing crops

futuristic very modern – as it might be in the future

habitat place where an animal or a plant lives

humid when there is a lot of water vapour in the air

immigrant someone who leaves their own country to settle in another

import buy in goods from other countries

irrigate artificially supply water for farming

land mass large, unbroken area of land

makeshift something that has been put together quickly

malaria disease spread by infected Anopheles mosquitoes

manioc type of root vegetable

marinated soaked in spices and flavourings before cooking

martial art form of self-defence, often practised as a sport or an art

open-cast mining where a large hole is dug rather than tunnelling underground to find minerals

plateau fairly high, flat area of land

poncho square or oblong piece of material with an opening for the head

rainforest warm, wet forest found in a tropical region

remote far from other places

resources things a country has that help it to make money

rural relating to the countryside

silt soil, mud, or clay that builds up in a river

species different types of animals and plants

summit highest point of a mountain

surdo bass drum that marks the beat of samba music

surveillance keeping something under close observation

Tropic of Capricorn imaginary line that marks 23° south of the Equator

welfare system scheme to help people with no money

Index

Titles in the *Destination Detectives* series include:

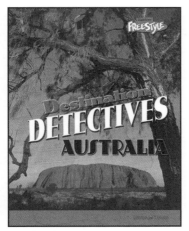

Hardback   1 406 20312 2

Hardback   1 406 20308 4

Hardback   1 406 20306 8

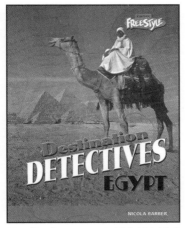

Hardback   1 406 20310 6

Hardback   1 406 20313 0

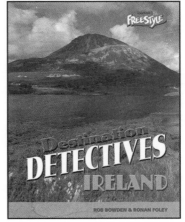

Hardback   1 406 20311 4

Hardback   1 406 20305 X

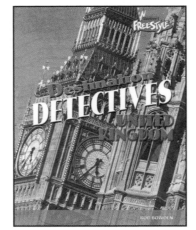

Hardback   1 406 20307 6

Hardback   1 406 20314 9

Find out about the other titles in this series on our website www.raintreepublishers.co.uk